Dick Hills was born in London in 1926, the fourth child in a family of five. He began script-writing in 1952 and, together with his former partner, Sid Green, wrote for such stars as Perry Como, Terry-Thomas, Bruce Forsyth and Morecambe and Wise. Dick and Sid then took their talents to America where they spent several very successful years. Disenchanted with Hollywood life, Dick Hills returned to England whilst Sid Green preferred to remain, thus ending their twenty-one-year partnership. More recently, Dick has written for Jimmy Tarbuck, Tommy Cooper, Frankie Howerd and Tom O'Connor, and also devised and presented *Tell Me Another* for Southern Television. Dick's interests include cricket, rugby and golf.

Also in this series

THE OFFICIAL IRISH JOKE BOOK
THE OFFICIAL IRISH JOKE BOOK NO 3 (BOOK 2 TO FOLLOW)
THE OFFICIAL SCOTTISH JOKE BOOK
THE WORLD'S WORST JOKE BOOK
THE OFFICIAL OZ JOKE BOOK
POSITIVELY THE LAST IRISH JOKE BOOK
THE OFFICIAL IRISH JOKE BOOK NO 4
THE OFFICIAL CAT LOVERS/DOG LOVERS JOKE BOOK
THE OFFICIAL BOOK OF BAWDY BALLADS
THE OFFICIAL ANGLER'S JOKE BOOK

Dick Hills

Delayed by Fog in Timbuctoo

A Book of Excuses

Illustrated by Bill Tidy

Futura Publications Limited

A Futura Book

First published in Great Britain by
Futura Publications Limited in 1979

This compilation copyright © Dick Hills 1979
Illustrations copyright © Bill Tidy 1979

ISBN 0 7088 1671 1

Printed by
William Collins Sons & Co. Ltd.
Glasgow

Futura Publications Limited
110 Warner Road, Camberwell
London SE5

Author's Note

I can honestly say that in twenty-five years of comedy writing I have only actually invented about six jokes of the 'Englishman, Irishman and Scotsman' variety. I do not know of any other writer who is an acknowledged source of original jokes of this kind. Jokes are not invented, they grow out of the soil, and very often the same ones come round again, tarted up to fit different occasions. No copyright is claimed on the material in this book, except the last two sections – 'Excuses for All Occasions' and 'The Excuse Book of Medical Terms'. I shall be happy to remunerate any reader who can prove that he is the original source of any joke appearing in this book.

Excuses . . . Excuses . . . Excuses . . .

Those who don't see the joke in the title of this book have to bear in mind that fog occurs in Timbuctoo about once in a thousand years. This is a book of jokes about excuses. It includes any joke in which the human worm can be detected trying to squirm off the hook. After all, the excuse, the cop-out, the cover-up, and the duck-out-from-under, are all forms of that escape clause we must have written into the contract of life in order to make it liveable. Without that clause, we would be swinging on the gibbet of guilt before the age of ten.

The very best of excuses are those which do not sound like excuses at all. My favourite is that of the Duke of Buckingham. (No evidence exists as to whether it was the one who stood on the bridge at Uckingham). The Duke was a Man About Town, but during the times of the Great Plague, he was forced to retreat to his country estate in Yorkshire until the plague abated. It was his first visit. He hated every minute of it. Unfortunately his household staff bent over backwards to attend to his every whim, and he

was embarrassed when he had to leave. Everyone was in tears. They begged him to return as soon as possible.

'Don't worry,' said the Duke. 'I shall be back at the very next Plague!' Most excuses however, are pretty lame, and are funny because they are lame. Like the shoplifter who was caught outside in the street wearing three suits.

'I just wanted to see what they look like in the light,' was his offering.

This little book hopes to make you chuckle, as you writhe under the thumb-screw of parental, marital, or gubernatorial inquisition. The special section at the end – 'Excuses for All Occasions' – is offered as a bit of life-saving material which might save the reader a divorce.

If your feeling is that divorces aren't worth saving, my excuse is that the excuses offered aren't all that good anyway.

DICK HILLS

Sexcuses

The social worker called on Flo Perkins and found her in tears.

'Me old man's left me and run orf to Canada!' she wailed.

'He didn't use that old excuse about your not satisfying him in bed did he?' asked the social worker, who thought she had solved that problem.

'No. He saw a notice saying "Drink Canada Dry" so he went!'

* * *

The randy overseas representative was having such a good time with the local girls in Tahiti, he searched for an excuse to stay longer. Eventually he sent a telegram to his wife: 'Staying another week – still buying.' This seemed to produce no repercussions, so at the end of the week he sent another telegram: 'Still buying.' Three days later he received a telegram back from his wife: 'Stay as long as you like – selling what you're buying.'

*　　*　　*

The young couple entered the doctor's surgery looking worried.

'It's like this, doc,' explained the young man, 'Doris and I are getting married in a month's time and we think there's something wrong with the way we're having intercourse.'

'I see,' said the doc. 'Well, I can't treat that problem under the National Health. It'll cost you £10 for a private consultation.'

'That's OK,' said the young man. 'Shall we show you how we're doing it?'

The doctor took up his note pad, 'Very well, if that's the way you want to proceed.' The young coupled undressed, climbed on to the doctor's examination couch and for five minutes thoroughly enjoyed themselves. The doctor snapped his notebook shut.

'Absolutely perfect,' he pronounced. 'I'm sorry to charge you £10, but I can't fault the way you're doing it.'

Nevertheless, the couple returned the next day, saying that they weren't happy with the doctor's diagnosis and repeated the performance, happily paying him another £10. This went on all week, and by the Friday the doctor was losing patience.

'Listen, I've told you there's nothing wrong with the way you are having intercourse!' he shouted angrily.' I've no objection to taking £10 off you every time if you're fools enough to pay it, but what possible excuse can you have for taking up a busy doctor's time and with a lot of sick people waiting?'

'It's like this, doc,' explained the young man. 'Doris can't sleep at my place, and I can't sleep at her place. It costs £30 a night in a hotel. But you only charge £10 and we get that back on B.U.P.A.!'

* * *

The Aussie carried his bride into the honeymoon suite, locked and bolted the door, and proceeded to empty the contents of the suitcases out of the window. Finally he took his new wife's entire wardrobe of dresses from the closet, threw them in the same direction and locked the window.

The bride burst into tears and pummelled him with her fists in anguish. 'You've just thrown my brand new trousseau into the muddy street! You're mad! I'll never forgive you for this! You've no excuse for treating me like this!'

'Don't worry, me little sheila,' grinned the Aussie

as he unbuckled his belt. 'By the time I let you out of here, those clothes will be out of fashion!'

* * *

The stockbroker's wife had a ready excuse when her husband returned home and found her in bed with a strange man.

'It's all right, my dear,' she said. 'I've gone public!'

* * *

The dolly bird tapped her escort on the shoulder as he slowed down the car.

'I said no excuses for stopping on the way home!'

'Exactly. I'm just curbing my emotions.'

* * *

The mother had just learned that her son had got himself a job as a fitter of underwear on models.

'I can't tell everybody that!' she gasped. 'What excuse can I give when the neighbours ask?'

'Just tell 'em,' responded her son with a grin, 'that when my business is good, it's wonderful – and when it's bad, it's still pretty good!'

* * *

A jealous husband hired a private detective to follow his wife and confirm what he suspected – that she was carrying on with another man. The detective reported that he followed her and a strange man to the cinema.

'Did you follow them inside?' asked the husband.

'No.'

'After all the money I pay you? Why not?'

'I'd already seen the picture,' replied the man.

* * *

Jim and Ron had been rivals for the hand of the delectable Daphne for a long time, but Ron was eventually the favoured suitor. He invited Jim to be the best man at the wedding, but Jim turned it down.

'What excuse can you give for not being the best man?' asked his mother sadly.

'Because I won't have a chance to prove it,' said Jim.

* * *

The marriage Guidance counsellor had a disgruntled couple in front of him. 'To be fair to you, Madam,' he conceded, 'your husband does apparently spend all his time watching football on the television. But why not discuss it with him sensibly? Why walk up and down in front of the television set with nothing on?'

'Well, it's like I said to him,' she replied. 'Either play with me or have me transferred!'

* * *

'Have you noticed old Albert's face lately? It's a mass of bruises!'

'Yes. His wife bashes him in bed.'

'Is that a fact? I wouldn't stand for my wife beating me up like that in bed.'

'He's got no excuse – he grins in his sleep!'

*   *   *

The hostess took the dizzy blonde wife to one side at the party.

'I ought to tell you that your husband is going round pinching all the women's bottoms, putting his hand up their skirts, and playing with their bosoms,' she said accusingly.

'Thank goodness!' sighed the girl, relieved, 'I thought it was just me!'

*   *   *

When a marriage has been staggering along for some years, it doesn't need much excuse for one partner to pack up and leave. Like the wife who decided to please her husband and lose weight. She suffered agonies walking around the house all day in one of the well-advertised weight-losing suits – an all-over transparent polythene outfit.

Her husband came home after work, took one look at her and groaned. 'Oh no. Not left-overs again!'

*   *   *

'*Divorce!*' echoed the matron at the Old People's Home. 'You and Stanley? I don't believe it. What on earth for? He's ninety and you're eighty-six!'

'Well,' sniffed the old girl, 'enough's enough!'

* * *

It was their silver wedding anniversary, and they decided to make a sentimental journey back to the hotel where they spent their honeymoon. They even booked the same room.

After a pleasant meal, with the odd glass or two of wine, they eventually retired to bed. The husband lay on his back, cupped his hands behind his head and stared reflectively at the ceiling.

'You know, dear,' he said, 'in all the years of our married life, there's one thing I've never forgiven you for.'

'Good gracious. What's that?' she said, startled.

'Well, if you remember – in this very same bed on our honeymoon night, I was just about to make love to you, and you jumped out of bed, packed your things and went back to your mother!' 'Oh that!' she said. 'But surely you can understand it. I was a young girl, only seventeen – I knew nothing about men. I just got very nervous and scared.'

'Ye-e-s, I suppose that explains it,' he said. He turned towards her. 'Shall we try again?'

* * *

'Why did you do those disgusting things with that young man in the front room last night?' bemoaned the mother. 'If you would only be a good girl, a nice man would come along.'

'But if you're a bad girl, Mother, a *lot* of them will!'

* * *

'Matilda! And you, Sir! Neither of you have an excuse for being found in this position. And keep *still* while I'm talking to you!'

* * *

'What's the idea?' demanded the nagging wife, brandishing a book at her husband. 'I found this under your pillow – '*A Hundred and One Risqué Stories!*'

'I thought it was a new novel by Risqué,' he replied with a shrug.

* * *

The daughter was dutifully reporting back to her mother over the telephone the details of her date with her first boyfriend.

'I hope you didn't go back to your flat with him,'

said the mother sharply. 'You know how your mother worries about you.'

'No. We went back to his flat,' the girl explained. 'And let his mother worry.'

* * *

The middle-aged couple went on their first holiday to the South of France. But the wife didn't realize how hot it would be until they got on the beach.

'Henry!' she announced imperiously, mindful of the chic French girls as they glided by in their scant bikinis. 'I have to go into town to buy something more suitable for the beach. Don't you dare move from this spot.'

'Of course not, my dear,' responded her husband.

When she returned an hour later, she was horrified to see Henry rolling in the sand with a tanned and topless beauty, hungrily kissing her breasts.

'Aaah, *chérie!*' breathed the girl huskily. *'Comme vous êtes beau! Quittons la plage! Quittez votre femme! Venez avec moi à mon apartiment fair l'amour quelques semaines!'*

'Henry!' barked the wife, prodding him with her umbrella. 'Explain yourself!'

'How can I?' snapped Henry. 'I don't know the bloody language!'

* * *

21

'What went on when you brought Jack back to the house last night?'

'We spent an hour in the loving room.'

'That's "*living*", Dora.'

'I'll say it is!'

*　　*　　*

'Prunella! Why have you got a painter in the house? You painted the bedroom yourself.'

'That's right, dear.'

'And why has he got his hand inside your panties?'

'Well, all I said to him was that I wanted him for a touch-up job, and to show him where you put your hand last night.'

*　　*　　*

'Listen,' explained the Marriage Guidance Counsellor patiently. 'I get dozens of genuine cases of broken marriages to patch up every day, and you come in and want advice on the first day of your honeymoon. You'd better have a good excuse, otherwise I'm going to report you for wasting my time.'

'Well, what would you think,' said the aggrieved

husband, 'if you got up after your honeymoon night and said "I feel like a new man ' and your bride said "And so do I"?'

* * *

'James! What is this *Playboy* centrefold doing under your pillow?'

'I didn't want anything to be squashed.'

* * *

'What's going on with you and your secretary?'

'Not much. Most of it comes off.'

* * *

A major drinking in the officers' mess thought he recognized a young lieutenant standing by the bar and went over and tapped him on the shoulder.

'You weren't by any chance serving in the British Army of the Rhine in 1969 were you?' The lieutenant took out a large diary and consulted it. '1967 India – 1968 Hong Kong – 1969 Germany. Yes, as a matter of fact I was.'

'Were you in Munich in August, by any chance?' went on the major, an edge creeping into his voice.

The young man consulted his diary again. 'Munich?

That would be under "M" – just a moment. Ah yes, I was. Quite right.'

'You didn't happen to sleep with a girl called Clovissa, did you?' 'Clovissa. That would be under "C" – now then – Annabel – Astrid – Beryl – Candy – Clovissa – yes, you're quite right. I did.' 'Well, she happens to be my wife,' exploded the major. *'And I don't like it!* Any excuse?'

The lieutenant consulted the back of his diary. 'Well, if it's any use – neither did I!'

* * *

'You promised the Church many sons, Mrs O'Shaughnessy,' said the priest. 'And you had one in 1969, 1970, 1971, 1972, 1973 and 1975. What happened to 1974? You would have received a commendation from the Pope.'

'Ah! 1974 . . . That was when me husband's business dropped off!'

* * *

Wife finds husband with the town flirt.

'Lionel! How could you!'

'Just watch and learn. Watch and learn!'

* * *

Paddy came home very late and very drunk one night, and when his wife asked him where he had been, he said he had attended the 38th Annual Reunion of the Irish Army Suicide Corps.

*   *   *

'We received an invitation to a dinner party at the Smythes' next week,' said Diedre to Charles when he returned from the office. 'But I don't think we should accept.'

'Why not, darling?'

'You're so *dull* at dinner parties, Charles, and you make me feel such a fool. You don't tell witty and mildly risqué stories like Bamber and Rodney do. It's such a let-down.'

For the next week, Charles racked his brains for a witty and mildly risqué story, but nothing came. Then by chance, at an office cocktail party, the Managing Director told a story that raised a big laugh but was also perfectly suitable for the drawing-room.

'This kid moved into the East End, you see,' explained the Managing Director to the mixed company. 'And the gang of kids in the locality said to him, "You're not Jewish". And he said "Oh yes, I am". And they said, "Oh no, you're not – prove it!" So the new kid said, "I'll give you proof".' At this point the Managing Director unzipped his trousers and fished inside. There was a chorus of small screams from the ladies present. Pulling out the tail of his shirt, the Manager Director went on, ' "Where else would you find a piece of shmutter like that?" ' The assembled company roared.

Delighted, Charles told Diedre to accept the invitation. 'I've got just the story,' he explained.

At the Smythes', without fail, both Bamber and Rodney regaled the guests with a fund of witty and mildly risqué stories. Charles was certain that his own was just right for the occasion and Diedre was looking at him expectantly. Charles tapped his coffee cup with his spoon and stood up. 'Just for once, I have a joke to tell,' he announced.

He told the story beautifully. His timing was perfect. But the wine must have been a little stronger than he had bargained for, and when he came to the tag, instead of taking out the end of his shirt, he produced his penis. ' "Where else would you find a piece of shmutter like that?" '

'He's not even Jewish,' observed Bamber.

'He's let me down again,' moaned Diedre.

'Why? Did he tell you he was?' quipped Rodney.

At the divorce court, Diedre said, 'There's no excuse for behaviour like that!'

And is there?

*　　*　　*

Mick was out late regularly every Monday night, conducting an affair with the local barmaid on her night off. His wife wanted to know what excuse he had for this regular absence from the home, and his reply is a model of intelligence and cunning which we would all do well to emulate in similar circumstances.

'Well,' he said, 'I'm tinkin' of adoptin' one of dem Vietnam babies, and I'm goin't to Chinese classes every Monday so's Oi knows what de kid is talkin' about when it grows up.'

* * *

'Our neighbour saw you out last night with a young girl,' accused the wife.

'There's a good reason for that,' replied the husband. 'My father gave me two pieces of advice for when I got married. First, always insist you spend one night a week out with the boys. Second, don't waste it on the boys!'

* * *

An arctic blizzard was blowing across the bleak Yorkshire moors when the travelling salesman banged on the farmhouse door and begged for shelter. The farmer welcomed him in but explained that he would have to share a bed with his son.

'Thanks all the same,' said the traveller, and turned back into the storm. The farmer chased after him and, grabbing him, yelled over the howl of the storm, 'What possible reason could you have for turning down my hospitality on a night like this?'

'I'm sorry,' the traveller shrieked back. 'But sharing a bed with your son! I'm in the wrong joke!'

*   *   *

The new vicar had only just taken up his duties when he was called upon by an old hag. Her figure was shrivelled, her clothes torn and dirty, and her whole body exuded a powerful odour. Despite her repulsive appearance, the dedicated vicar regarded her as one of his flock and listened patiently to her tale of woe. Her husband had deserted her, leaving six children in her care.

'How old are you, madam?' he enquired.

'Twenty-eight,' replied the crone.

Secretly, the parson thought the husband was justified in leaving a wife who had allowed herself to degenerate into such a foul-smelling bag of bones. But over the next few months he diligently tracked him down, conducted all the legal arrangements on behalf of the woman, and thus eventually restored her right to proper maintenance.

No sooner had he completed these affairs, than she called on him again, looking even more repulsive, and complaining that the lodger had put her in the family way and done a bunk.

The vicar's saint-like patience snapped. 'Dammit, woman! After all the trouble you've let yourself in for, and after all the hard work I've done to gain you restitution — ! What possible excuse can you have for letting a man take you like that?'

She smiled wanly, showing her two remaining black teeth. 'I thought it was rather nice of him to ask!'

* * *

'I know this is a desolate region,' said the District Commissioner to the Government Agent. 'But that's no excuse for having sexual relations with an emu. We are still officially a British Colony and there are certain standards of behaviour to be observed. Do you want to say anything before I make my report?'

'Oh hell,' said the Agent. 'I'll marry the damn bird.'

*   *   *

'I've just come back from the Women's Guild,' announced the domineering wife to her husband. 'And they are all telling the story about the incident in the men's sauna bath yesterday. It's made me an absolute laughing-stock!'

'I've got a feeling,' said her husband, 'that I'm going to get the blame for this. All right, what did they say?'

'They said that a young girl walked into the men's room by mistake and all the men quite properly grabbed their towels and covered their private parts. All except _you_, Cedric! You used your towel to cover your face! There's absolutely no excuse!'

'Oh yes, there is,' he smiled. 'I know how _I'm_ recognized!'

*   *   *

'Can't you see that No Smoking sign, young man!'

'Oh sorry. It's just a habit.'

'Habits can be cured. My husband hasn't put a cigarette in his mouth for twenty years.'

'Really? I've never put it anywhere else!'

*　*　*

'I can understand your anger at finding your wife in bed with another man, but why did you shoot her?'

'Well, your Honour, it saves me shooting a different man each week.'

*　*　*

'Why didn't you stick up for me when those louts kicked sand all over me? You're just a 7½-stone weakling!'

'True. But once I took a Charles Atlas course and built myself up from a 7½-stone weakling to a 12½-stone Adonis.'

'I would love you if you were.'

'And have a 17½-stone hulk come along and kick sand in my face?'

*　*　*

'Oh no! Not again!' muttered the exhausted husband, as he woke up to find his nymphomaniac wife's hand starting to wander. 'You agreed with the doctor when he said we are having too much of it. And you agreed only to have sex on days of the week with an "R" in them, so you've got no excuse.'

'Yes, I have,' she murmured silkily. 'It's Mondray!'

* * *

Then there was the case of the young man who fell out of bed in a state of complete physical exhaustion. 'Come on, baby,' said the girl, grabbing him. 'Don't you want to live?'

'Yes,' he groaned. 'But what will I do if I survive?'

* * *

Some lucky culprits have an excuse handed to them on a plate. Like the wife who was found in bed with her lover, whose husband exclaimed, 'What the hell do you think you're doing?'

'I told you he was stupid!' She said to her lover.

* * *

The copper had suspected for a long time that a shifty stall-owner on the corner was dealing in pornography. When he saw the suspect furtively hand over a photograph to a customer, he moved in quickly.

'Just as I thought,' he said, studying the picture. 'Pornography.'

'Pornography?' uttered the trader with feigned amazement. 'Blimey! Haven't you ever seen a picture of nine people in love before?'

* * *

'Now I've finally got you alone,' breathed the wolf as he grappled with his 'score' for the night in the back of the car, 'you won't co-operate. What's the idea?'

'When two's company,' she said, fighting back, '*three*'s often the result!'

* * *

'All right, let's have it!' demanded the termagant of a wife, brandishing a rolling-pin, as soon as her hen-pecked husband crept down for breakfast. 'When I cried out in my sleep last night "It's my husband!", why did you jump straight out of bed and hide in the wardrobe?'

'But my dear,' he said, 'I didn't want to interrupt anything you were doing!'

* * *

'Hallo, darling,' said the husband over the phone. 'Sorry I didn't get home last night. I was belting down the M1 – dead keen to get back to you, m'dear – and I had a blow-out and had to spend the night at a motel.'

'It must have been a big one. The police have just called to say they've picked up your briefcase in a Strip Club in Soho!'

* * *

She was the most beautiful and most desirable woman in Southern Italy. Sex oozed from every pore. He was handsome and rich. The marriage was written in the stars. But he did not consummate the union.

'Why? Why?' she cried.

'*Carissima*,' he sighed, 'I must confess to you. My entire reproductive apparatus was shot off in the war.'

'Excuses! Excuses!' she wailed.

* * *

The luxury cruiser struck a coral reef in the South Seas and sunk without trace. Only the handsome First Mate and a honeymoon couple survived, and struggled through the waves to a desert island.

During the cruise, the First Mate had taken a strong fancy to the young bride, especially as the husband was a weedy-looking type, and so he prepared his excuse well beforehand.

'Now the first thing we have to do,' he said, briskly taking command, 'Is to build a signal fire. Luckily I've saved the ship's binoculars. So we take it in turns to watch from the top of that big palm tree, and keep a look-out for passing ships.'

'Oh yeah?' said the husband suspiciously, pulling his nubile spouse closer. 'And who's going up there first?'

'I shall, of course!' said the First Mate brightly. He climbed briskly up the palm tree whilst the pair built a fire and sat disconsolately in the sand.

After about ten minutes scanning the horizon, the First Mate shouted down to them below. 'Stop that screwing!'

'What did he say?' asked the scandalized husband. The young bride blushed and pretended she hadn't heard. From then on, every ten minutes throughout his four-hour watch, the First Mate shouted down to them. 'Will you stop that screwing!' At the end of the watch, he descended and handed the husband the binoculars.

'Your turn!' he smiled.

'All right,' said the other. 'But I want you both sitting right under this tree where I can see you.'

'Of course,' said the First Mate, smiling again. The husband climbed the palm tree with difficulty and for ten minutes sedulously scanned the horizon. He looked down, and then leaned farther over, frowning in disbelief. 'He's right,' he muttered. 'It does look like screwing from up here!'

* * *

Charlie had every intention of getting home early, to put in a bit of credit with the wife. But when he got to the pub he found that he had won the football sweep. One drink led to another, and in no time at all his cronies had dragged him off to a local dive where they drank and debauched with the obliging female staff until the early hours.

'I don't know how I'm gonna get out of thish one, Arthur,' sighed Charlie as they staggered up to his front door.

'Here,' said Arthur, 'put this bit o' chalk behind your ear and tell the wife the whole truth. You'll have no worries.'

Charlie was too smashed to argue. He lurched into the bedroom and his wife shot up in bed and yelped. 'Where the hell have you been?'

'I went into town and got drunk, and then I went on to a club and got drunker, and then I jumped into bed with a lady of the town and screwed the arse off her,' Charlie confessed.

'Don't give me that,' said his wife sarcastically, catching sight of the chalk behind his ear. 'You've been out playing darts all evening. I know you!'

* * *

After four years in a convent, seven years at Rhodean, and three years at a finishing school in Switzerland, all under the watchful eyes of her protective parents, Phoebe's libido was beginning to make loud complaining noises. So on the first day that she officially started work as a secretary, she hooked up with the lecherous office boy. After the usual meal and dance, she suggested going somewhere quiet. So he took her to the local cemetery, stripped off her clothes, laid her on a tomb and gave her a good one. On the way home she prepared her excuse.

Her mother was waiting in her bedroom. 'I don't know where you've been. But straight into the bath with you, young lady!' As Phoebe stripped off she said, 'Oh mother, I went to a very high-class yoga symposium. They teach you how to make every part of your body come alive!'

'Really,' said her mother, eyeing her daughter's nude body. 'Did you know your backside died in 1884?'

* * *

The son-in-law ran his hands through his hair in final anguish and said to Mrs Murphy: 'I'm sorry, but I'm divorcing your daughter.'

'Holy Mother of Mary!' exclaimed the lady. 'And why is that?'

'I was in Holland last week on business,' said the husband. 'I sent a telegram to Maureen saying I'd be home on the Saturday. And when I walked in, there she was on the bed, underneath another man!'

'Oh deary me, deary me!' Mrs Murphy wrung her hands. 'Don't do anything rash. Give me a chance to talk to her. There may be a reason.'

'Well, all right,' he muttered reluctantly, 'but just a week.'

At the end of the week Mrs Murphy came up to him full of smiles. 'Everything is fine. You can go back home. She had a perfectly good reason. She didn't receive your telegram!'

*   *   *

'Why are you so damned ugly?' he asked his blind date.

She thought desperately for an answer.

'I was a very beautiful baby, but I was exchanged by gypsies!'

*   *   *

'Why did you shoot your husband?'

'I don't believe in divorce!'

*   *   *

'I slapped my boyfriend in the face last night.'

'I hate that. There's no excuse for groping.'

'No, it was just to see if he was awake!'

*   *   *

'You've no excuse for punching my wife in the face!'

'Yes, I have. I've found out she's been unfaithful to both of us!'

* * *

Mrs O'Flaherty: A man can talk as much as he likes, Mrs Finnegan, but there's no way he can excuse infidelity, I'm thinking.

Mrs Finnegan: You're right, you're right.

Mrs O'Flaherty: Talking of infidelity – d'you not see Mrs O'Patrick over there? She's putting it about that there's only one woman in the whole street who's been faithful to her husband.

Mrs Finnegan: She isn't!

Mrs O'Flaherty: She is!

Mrs Finnegan: There's no excuse for that either.

Mrs O'Flaherty: There isn't.

Mrs Finnegan: No, indeed . . . I wonder which one it is?

* * *

The Local Women's Liberation Chairperson finished off her address to the gathered housewives thus:

'And finally, if your husband has a failing, stop making excuses for him! Give it to him right between the eyes!'

Mrs Smithers took this advice to heart. That evening her husband arrived home from the bank as usual, and found his wife writhing naked in bed with a dirty unshaven stranger.

'Agatha! What's the meaning of this?' he yapped.

Mrs Smithers smoothed her hair and said calmly: 'He's an old tramp, dear, and he came begging for a coat. So I gave him an old coat of yours. Then I gave him an old shirt, and an old pair of boots, and an old hat. And he said to me, "Is there anything else you can give me that your husband hasn't any use for?"'

* * *

'Why do you want to marry *him*, of all people?'

'Well, I reckon that if they can make penicillin out of mouldy bread, I can make something out of him!'

* * *

The Dublin solicitor said to Mrs O'Connor, 'You might want to divorce your husband, but you still have to supply grounds. For example, can you sue him for desertion?'

'Desertion?' exclaimed Mrs O'Connor. 'And how could I get Paddy on desertion when I can't even get him out of the house? Can I sue him for not stirring out of the armchair from morn till night?'

'No, no!' said the solicitor irritably. 'What about cruelty?'

'Cruelty! Me darling Paddy wouldn't hurt the hair on a fly's leg. He's as gentle as a lamb and treats me like a queen, and has loved me every night since the day we were married.'

'Hmm,' muttered the legal man, disgruntled. 'In that case it's a waste of time. And from the way you're carrying on, I'd say you don't want to divorce your husband at all.'

'But what about infidelity?' posed Mrs O'Connor suddenly.

'Infidelity? But you said he made love to you every night.'

'Indeed he does. But I'm certain he ain't the father of me second child!'

*   *   *

'Put your foot down, Ethel!'

'You're joking, Mavis! It's pouring down.'

'What's that got to do with it?'

'Well, there's no excuse for breaking the speed limit – and the grass is too wet to buy-off the coppers!'

*   *   *

'Alastair! You said you wouldn't.'
    'No. I said I couldn't'.
    'But you can. And you are'.
    'I told you you weren't like other girls.'

                    *   *   *

The vicar looked at the octogenarian bride and groom.
    '*Why?*' he asked the best man.
    '*How?*' responded he.

Any Excushe ish Better than None!

'I thought you said that when you came out of the army you'd give up drink?'

'Oh, didn't I tell you? I joined the navy.'

* * *

'Drunk again,' commented the Magistrate, eyeing the bedraggled Paddy in the dock. 'I suppose you have an excuse, the same as always?'

'In trute, me Lordship, I only drink to ease de pain in me heart. I was shot roit dere in de war.'

'Poppycock, man!' snapped the beak. 'If you were shot in the heart you would be dead.'

Ah, but me heart was in me mouth at the toim!'

* * *

'Another night round the pub boozing all evening –
What's the excuse this time?'

'Well, there I wash! With a drink in my handsh, in
front of a blazing fire. It wash very difficult to leave.'

'You could always get up and walk out!'

'With all thoshe firemen in the way?'

*   *   *

'I'm inclined to believe the constable,' said the same beak in dealing with the next case of D & D. 'He saw you staggering about the street, and then you threw a cat across the road. There's no way you can explain yourself out of that one'.

'I insist,' said the defendant, 'that I was perfectly sober. I wasn't staggering – I was positioning myself to catch the cat, because it looked as if it was going to fall off the tree. I happen to be a first-class cricketer.'

'Assuming you caught it, why did you throw it across the road?' asked the Magistrate.

'Pure instinct. I field at cover point and I returned it to the wicket-keeper.'

* * *

'I thought you said you never drink before noon?'
'It's noon in Bangkok!'

* * *

There's one thing about alcohol – when you've consumed just the right amount, it helps you to think quickly. Like the husband who was caught drinking in a pub after he had sworn to his wife that he had gone on the waggon.

'So your pledge means nothing!' she rasped.

'Not at all, my dear. You see, when I drank regularly, I always had one scotch for myself, and one for my dear old army pal Fred, who was killed in the war – just for sentimental reasons. Now I'm on the waggon, I have to force myself and drink Fred's!'

* * *

'Is there any excuse for that George Drinkwell? Look at him – lying there face down in the gutter at ten in the morning.'

'Still less excuse for his wife – she's looking up at him!'

* * *

The young man staggered over to the bar in a state of alcoholic euphoria. 'I've got three dolly birds over there who're mine for tonight. Give us – *hic* – three large gins, Miss!'

'Don't you "Miss" me!' snapped the busty wench tartly.

'OK. Make that four large gins, then!'

* * *

'I've got used to you coming home drunk every Friday,' hissed the wife as she went through his pockets. 'But what excuse have you got for spending every penny of your wages?'

'Oh . . . Ah! I bought shomthing for the housh, my shweet.'

'What did you buy for the house worth £90?'

'Er . . . Ten rounds of drinks!'

* * *

The bride had no excuse at all for consuming more than the appropriate amount of wine at the wedding reception, and was rather unsteady when she rose to say her few words. She stared glassy-eyed at a gift coffee-percolator. 'Oh yes,' she giggled. 'I'd like to thank my mum and dad-in-law for giving me such a perky copulator!'

* * *

Man is a feeble creature, and often feels compelled to make excuses, even when circumstances are stacked up against him. Take the sensational case at the Old Bailey in which drink had been the root cause of a man's depravity.

Summing up, the judge said: 'It has been proved that you consumed enormous amounts of alcohol every day; that you threw a dozen women into the canal; that you set fire to at least six premises; that you vandalized scores of cars, despoiled people's property, and perpetrated numberless despicable minor offences, including throwing four pug dogs into a cement-mixer. Have you anything to say before I pronounce judgement?'

'Well,' muttered the prisoner in a hurt tone, 'I wanted to get into the Guinness Book of Records for *something*!'

* * *

As he walked through the gates of Heaven with St Peter, the young man decided it was the one moment in his life to be truthful. 'I should really be in Hell,' he confessed. 'All my life I've smoked a hundred cigarettes and drunk four bottles of scotch a day. I was a permanent drunk and ruined many a woman as a result. I've got no excuse for being here at all.'

'Oh, I don't think it matters,' said St Peter. 'We've got nothing like that up here anyway!'

* * *

The hatchet-faced wife was a devoted do-gooder, and her poor hen-pecked husband was usually the first victim of her reforming zeal. Most recently she had gone in for teetotalism.

'Lionel,' she pronounced one evening, 'I'm glad you arrive home every night perfectly sober, but why do you always bring a crowd of drunken friends back with you?'

'Revenge, my dear,' he replied. 'One look at you and they take the pledge.'

* * *

Men have always got two good excuses for staying out drinking all night. Either they've got no wives to go home to, or they have.

* * *

'Every time we go to a restaurant with friends, you pass out and have to be carried home. What's your excuse for that?'

'Well, that way I'm always out for the count when the bill arrives!'

*   *   *

The new overseas agent had heard about the drinking ban in the Middle East and so he secreted a bottle of scotch under his coat. Unfortunately, just as he was passing through Customs, the bottle developed a leak.

'What iss dat, pliss?' accused the swarthy official, pointing to the brown drip.

'A panther puppy,' said the quick-witted agent.

*   *   *

'Don't make your pals carry the can for getting you drunk.'

'They not only carry the can, they carry me as well.'

Jobs, Bosses and other Exec-scuses!

Mr Peabody was considered throughout the department as spineless and sycophantic. But on this Monday morning he strode purposefully through the office with head held high and burst into the boss's office.

'Peabody! What is the meaning of this?' his outraged superior demanded. Peabody responded with a cynical smirk.

'I just want to tell you, Mr Ponsonby-bleeding-Smythe, that in the thirty years I've worked in this firm I've never come across such a snide, arrogant, pompous and mean-minded bastard – '

'Peabody! You've taken leave of your senses!' barked Smythe, pressing the bell for the Security man.

' – Such a heartless, big-headed little Hitler –' continued Peabody.

'Peabody! I give you just one chance to provide yourself with an excuse!'

'I don't need an excuse, pal,' leered Peabody. 'On Saturday night I sent you a letter of resignation. And why? Mr Ponson-bloody-by Smythe? Because I've won the pools, that's why. One hundred thousand smackers. And you'll find my letter on your desk. Because I've never suffered so much from a jumped-up, poncey, dictator, such an evil pot-mess of crap calling himself a human being, such a putrid collection of skin an bone as – '

'This isn't your letter of resignation,' frowned his employer. 'This is your pools coupon entry'.

' – as our tea-boy! And I think I can do his job better,' concluded Peabody.

* * *

'Not fired *again*!' bewailed the long-suffering house-wife. 'What happened this time?'

The hapless and jobless husband sighed. 'I don't know why I said it. But when the boss offered me coffee, I said "No thanks, coffee keeps me awake".'

* * *

'You've been late four times in a row, O'Rooke!'
'And they said I could never learn anything, Sir!'

* * *

The Efficiency Expert checked his list and then called in the Floor Manager. 'I just want you to take a look at your production output figures, Carrington,' he said, handing the man a graph. 'They show a marked fall over the past three months, for which you are responsible. I'm a reasonable man, and if you've got a good excuse I won't recommend that you be demoted.'

'I'm sorry, Sir,' mumbled Carrington. 'I can't concentrate on my job. I've been having these terrible nightmares.'

'What sort of nightmares?'

'Every night I dream that my wife and Raquel Welch are fighting over me – and the wife keeps winning!'

*　*　*

'Parkinson, I have interviewed a lot of prospective employees over the last weeks and every one has demanded exorbitant wages. Eventually I tracked it down to you. What's the idea of going around saying I pay you twice as much as I actually do?'

'To protect your good name, Sir.'

*　*　*

Two tramps were comparing notes on their progress since they last met.

'I blame the present government,' said the first.

'You must be kidding,' said the other. 'Under the last government you were a tramp!'

* * *

The American couple were on a return visit to Stonehenge. 'What excuse have they got for that, Elmer?' Sadie asked her husband.

'Excuse? Why do they need an excuse? That's Stonehenge.'

'Typical British workmen, I'd say. They haven't done a thing to the place since we were here last!'

*   *   *

'I know I said I was always looking for a responsible job, dear. But every time something goes wrong they hold me responsible!'

*   *   *

'And why have you lost your union card?'

'Jealousy. I spent so much time lolling about, the lads thought I was the foreman!'

*   *   *

The irate patient burst into the doctor's surgery. 'I happen to know that you are treating me and my next-door neighbour for the same complaint – nervous debility. You gave him pills, and you gave me pills too. Why is it that *his* pills make him dream all night of screwing all the girls in the Miss World Contest, and *my* pills make me dream of carrying two hundred-weight sacks of spuds up a bloody great hill?'

'Ah!' explained the doc. 'He's a private patient and your on the National Health!'

'Well, in that case I'll pay the extra money and have his pills,' decided the man.

Within a week his boss called him in and gave him the sack. 'I can't keep you on,' he told him. 'You fall down exhausted as soon as you walk into the office.'

'It's my dreams,' blubbered the victim. 'Every night I dream of screwing all the girls in the Miss World Contest, and then I have to carry two hundred-weight sacks up a bloody great hill!'

* * *

Then there was the circus showman. His excuse for firing his own wife out of the cannon was that it saved one fare back home.

* * *

'Why did you chuck your job in, Dolores?' asked one curvaceous blonde of another.

'The boss was only interested in one thing,' said the other. 'My typing!'

* * *

'The main requirement in your job,' said the Sales Chief, 'is that you provide your own car. Now I find out you're trying to do the job on foot. What's happened to your car?'

'I had this terrible back trouble, Sir,' explained the employee, 'And my wife took me to this acupuncturist. He said he would have me up and walking in three weeks. And he was right. I had to sell my car to pay his bill!'

*   *   *

There was the case of the poor fellow starting his first day as Assistant Stage Manager in a ritzy night-club. Cueing in the opening dance number, he yelled, 'Right! Enter soubrette with candle left upper entrance!' And the chorus line laughed so much as they danced on that all their tits fell out and the place was closed.

*   *   *

'I bet you needed a good excuse last night!' said the bachelor gleefully to his married companion, having dumped him on his doorstep at three o'clock in the morning.

'I was lucky,' the other explained. 'When I crept

into the bedroom the wife said "Is that you Rover?" '

'What did you do?'

'I'm not daft. I panted a bit and gave her hand a lick.'

* * *

There are those rare moments when no excuse is needed for our behaviour. Like the plumber who kept on contracting occupational diseases and complaints. No matter how bad he was, his doctor would give him no more than the usual advice over the phone. One night, it was the doctor's turn to call the plumber.

'I know it's two in the morning,' he shouted down the line. 'But the main's burst and the kitchen's full of water.'

'Chuck two aspirins down the sink every four hours,' advised the plumber, 'and if it's no better in the morning, give me a call!'

* * *

The boss spotted his truant office-boy at the football match. He leaned forward and tapped him on the shoulder.

'So this is your uncle's funeral!' he observed with biting sarcasm.

'It will be in a minute, Sir,' replied the boy without hesitation. 'He's the referee.'

* * *

'I keep telling you,' protested the husband in response to his wife's nagging. 'It's useless going down to the Labour Exchange. Jobs are scarce. They're only giving work to school-leavers. Do I look like a school-leaver? I'm thirty years old!'

'Can't you tell them you were kept in?'

* * *

'Why are you such a weak-willed, easily-dominated Yes-man, Jones?' asked the boss one day.

'It's the wife, sir, I'm afraid,' spluttered Jones.

'Never mind. You make an ideal right-hand man!'

* * *

'What are you having to drink, Jim?' invited Mike as his pal walked into the pub.

'I'm not drinking any more with you, mate. I don't

drink with wife-bashers. I saw Flo yesterday, she had a right pearler.'

'Listen, Jim,' explained his pal. 'All my married life I've had to put up with the old business of keeping up with the Joneses next door. When the Joneses got a colour telly, *we* had to have one. When the Joneses got a deep-freeze, *we* had to have a deep-freeze. Then it was a set of original prints, a three-week cruise on the *QE2*, double-glazing, solar heating, a sauna bath and a swimming pool. All because of the Joneses. And then I found out. The wife had been telling the Joneses what to buy next so she had an excuse for saying we ought to buy it. So I laid one on her.'

'The drinks are on me, pal,' said Jim.

* * *

She was a card fanatic, and the sessions went on later and later every night. One particular school went on until three o'clock in the morning. So as not to wake her husband, she took all her clothes off in the hall and tiptoed up to the bedroom. The husband opened one eye and saw the naked figure.

'Lost again, I see,' he muttered.

* * *

'Pull the other one, it's got bells on!' said the boss scornfully to his Irish workman. 'Are you trying to tell me you're an hour late because it was so icy under foot that every time you took one pace forward you slipped two paces back? At that rate you'd never get here at all.'

'So I wouldn't, Sorr – if I hadn't turned round and walked the other way!'

* * *

Harold was tall and handsome, but his pretty fiancée wouldn't marry him unless he held down a regular job. His excuse was that he was always the victim of bad luck.

'There's no such thing as *repeated* bad luck,' she pronounced primly.

'If you don't believe me, come down to the Dock Gates Arms with me tonight,' he invited. 'I've got the offer of a job as a bouncer. I'm sure to get taken on unless I have bad luck, because I'm the only one big enough around here to handle that mob.'

They arrived there about nine o'clock when the boozing was in full swing. Already there had been a couple of fights. Broken glasses littered the floor. Harold introduced himself to the man behind the bar.

'You look the type,' said the harrassed bartender. 'Let's see you in action.'

Harold took off his jacket, went up to the biggest and loudest-mouthed drunk, tapped him on the shoulder and said 'Oi! You! – out!' The big man started to protest but Harold picked him up like a baby and slung him through the pub window.

'Do I get the job?' he asked the bartender.

'Well, I can't actually hire you myself,' said the other. 'You'll have to ask the guv'nor.'

'Which one is he?' asked Harold.

'You've just slung him out of the window,' said the bartender.

Excuse me for Growing up!

'You're very late home from school,' said the worried mother to her teenage daughter. 'What's your excuse this time?'

'The boy who was following me walked very slowly,' said the daughter.

* * *

The cockney kid sniffed, wiped his nose on his sleeve, and approached his mum.

"Ere, Mum – you know that vase you're always worried abaht in case it gits smashed?'

'Wot abaht it?'

'Yer worries is over!'

* * *

The small boy lost his mother in the supermarket. 'Rosemary!' he bawled. 'Where are you, Rosemary?'

His mother came up and gave her son a cuff. 'What will the other people think – calling me Rosemary!' she scolded. 'If you want me, just call Mummy.'

'But the place is full of Mummies,' wailed her son.

*　　*　　*

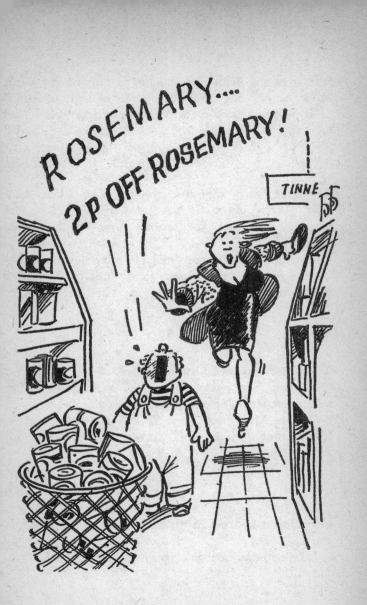

'What excuse have you hooligans got for throwing bricks at my dog and scaring the life out of him?'

'If we was better shots, Missus, we'd 'it 'im!'

*   *   *

'I've told you a thousand times to comb your hair after playing football!' said the mother. 'Look at yourself! You look an absolute mess! What's your excuse this time?'

The small urchin searched his mind for a second. 'There were so many heads in the mirror, I think I must have combed the wrong one!' he offered.

*   *   *

There's no answer to some excuses.

'You're late again, Priscilla,' reprimanded her schoolteacher. 'You *must* start out earlier!'

'Please, Miss!' explained Priscilla with all sincerity, 'By the time I left for school, it was too late to start out earlier!'

*   *   *

One Hollywood kid in the park gave the other one a push.

'My pop can beat your pop!' he challenged.

74

'No, he can't!' shouted the other.

'Yes, he can!'

'No, he can't!'

'Yes, he can!'

'No, he can't, you fool. Your pop *is* my pop!'

* * *

The English Master exploded in utter rage. 'May I remind you, Etherington, that I set you an essay on an imaginary game of cricket – and you've produced nothing! Before I tan the hide off you, I shall be interested to hear your excuse.'

'Rain stopped play, Sir.'

* * *

'Come along, Frederick, it's time to go to school.'

'I don't want to go to school!'

'What excuse is it this time?'

'I hate school. I hate it. I hate it. I *hate* it!'

'But Frederick – you must go to school. You're the Headmaster!'

* * *

'In olden days,' the teacher reminded her class, 'it was barbarianism. Then it was imperialism. Then it was democratic socialism. What is it today, Paul?'

'Monday, Miss.'

* * *

There are some excuses that leave schoolteachers breathless. The Maths master was reprimanding young Harris for not doing his homework. 'I told you to ask your parents for help if you found it too difficult. The problem was: if it takes 5 men 3 days to dig a garden of $4\frac{1}{2}$ acres, what size garden would be dug by 10 men in 4 days working at the same rate? Didn't you ask your father, Harris?'

'Yes, Sir. He said if anyone had a garden that size he'd report 'em to the local council, and you'd never find 10 men to dig it up anyway, and even if you did, the union would blackleg them for working too fast!'

* * *

Little Samantha would look for any excuse to stay up late, and when she heard that company was expected that evening, she asked her mother if she might play her party piece on the piano.

'Samantha, you're going to bed at your usual time and that's the end of it!' said her mother. When her father returned from work, she tried the same suggestion on him, but without success. So Samantha switched to the 'sobbing-and-sulking' technique. Eventually her mother made a concession. 'If you get yourself washed and ready for bed, I'll let you say grace for us all before you go to bed,' she promised.

The assembled company were seated round the dining-table waiting, when the small daugher was ushered in.

'What do I say, Mummy?' she whispered.

'Just say what Daddy says at breakfast, dear,' her mother prompted.

Samantha closed her eyes and said: 'Dear God! We're not having those terrible people round to dinner *again*, are we?'

* * *

'As you all know, children, America was discovered by Christopher Columbus . . .' began the teacher.

'Please, Miss!' interrupted the class know-all, raising his hand. 'My father's a research Professor in history, and he says America was discovered long before Columbus!'

'That's quite true,' admitted the teacher, searching for an excuse. 'But before Columbus, it had always been hushed up.'

* * *

The policeman tapped the loiterer on the shoulder.

'I've been watching you. It's three o'clock in the morning and you've been mooching back and forth past these houses for an hour. What's the idea?'

The man explained. 'You see, I've lost my front door key and I'm waiting for my teenage kids to come home and let me in!'

* * *

Twelve-year-old Percy, who had a leaning towards crime stories and TV cop series, wrote up his account of the Gunpowder Plot as follows: 'So Guido decided he couldn't make it on his own, so he called his mob in Vegas who called in the syndicate boys. There was Flywheel Fred, the best get-away man in the business, Hair-trigger Luigi, the best hit man on the Coast, and Jelly Giovanni, the best powder man – Jelly could blow the wart off a tart's nose without making her sneeze. Just when they got the whole caper put together to blow the G-boys to Kingdom Come, some Mouth grassed and they were taken out on the job by the Feds.'

His mother read it through and gave her son a clout.

'That's one from me, and I hope your teacher gives you another. It sounds nothing like the story of Guy Fawkes!'

'Aw!' said the boy unrepentant. 'The way the teacher described it, they wouldn't have got half-way across Westminster Bridge!'

* * *

'Why are you late for your first day at School?' rasped the Headmaster to the new boy.

'Please, Sir, I met a gang of kids who said they were going to throw bricks in the river.'

'That's no excuse!' barked the Head.

'Please, Sir, I'm Brix!' said the boy. 'I had to go home and change.'

* * *

It was seven-year-old Robin's birthday. A mixed gathering of children and mothers were enjoying the cakes and jellies.

'Please, Mum,' said Robin, 'I'm going to fart.' There was a moment of horrified silence. Then his mother smacked him soundly.

'Robin! You naughty boy! Keep that sort of thing to yourself!'

'But when Dad does that,' he bawled through his tears, 'You always say, "You might give us a bit of warning" '.

Petscuses!

Johnnie's mother was furious when she discovered he had taken out their new poodle puppy and sold it to a stranger.

'Do you realize that puppy cost Daddy £40?' she raged. 'A stranger wouldn't pay all that money to a small boy – what did you sell him for?'

'For chewing up my aeroplane,' sobbed Johnnie.

* * *

A country lady was attacked and robbed in her home.

'It's not really my business,' observed the Inspector as he took notes. 'But in a lonely place like this you really need a man about the house. You're still young and attractive enough to get yourself a husband.'

The lady sniffed contemptuously. 'I've got a dog that snores, a parrot that swears, and a cat that stays out all night. What do I want a husband for?'

* * *

'Couldn't you go any faster?' complained the owner to the jockey, after his favourite horse had come in last.

'Of course,' said the jockey. 'But you're supposed to stay on the horse.'

* * *

The RSPCA man called on Mr Turner.

'It's been reported by the neighbours that you have been cutting all the tails off your puppies.'

'That's right,' nodded the dog owner. 'My mother-in-law is paying us a visit and I don't want anyone to show she's welcome.'

*   *   *

'Stop pulling the cat's tail, Tommy!'

'I'm just standing on it. He's doing the pulling!'

*   *   *

The housewife took the cat back to the pet shop.

'You said this cat was a good mouser,' she complained. 'I want my money back. I found him playing with three mice in the cellar this morning.'

'Ah! That's because they were *your* mice,' explained the pet shop owner. 'If a strange one came in, he'd have him!'

*   *   *

The story was reported in the newspapers some years ago, of the motorist who was stopped by a police patrol. A hit-and-run had been reported and the car fitted the description exactly. It was a green Ford with a large dent in the front bonnet. The police thought that they had caught their man.

'Would you like to explain how your car came to be damaged, Sir?' asked the officer.

'An elephant sat on it,' replied the motorist, very deap-dan.

'Yes, highly risible, Sir,' nodded the officer sarcastically. 'I think you'd better come with us to the station.'

'Take a look at that if you don't believe me,' said the motorist, offering the officer a sheet of paper. It was an insurance claim signed by a circus-owner admitting liability. Apparently the motorist had been driving through a local High Street and had come up without warning in the rear of a circus parade, at the end of which was a large elephant. The motorist slowed down and proceeded at a respectable distance. Then, suddenly, the elephant stopped, backed a little, and sat down on the bonnet of the car.

*　　*　　*

Then there was the little lad who, when asked why he was teaching his dog to wag his tail up and down instead of from side to side, explained that he lived in a very small house.

*　　*　　*

A man entered a butcher's shop with his mongrel. The dog snatched a piece of prime beef off the counter and shot out of the door.

'Oi! Is that your dog?' shouted the butcher.

'It used to be,' said the man quickly, 'but it fends for itself now!'

*   *   *

Then there was the butcher who was serving his customers one morning when a Labrador trotted in with a piece of paper in his mouth. On the paper, the message was written: 'Dear butcher, please give Kim two pounds of sausages and I will pay you later. Mrs Briggs.' The butcher gave the sausages to the dog, who dutifully trotted out with them. Later, the owner came into the shop and paid for the sausages.

'Smart dog you've got,' observed the butcher. This went on for several weeks, and after a time the butcher didn't bother to read the message, he merely supplied Kim with the sausages. But Mrs Briggs ceased to appear, and the butcher started to worry about the large sausage bill building up. Eventually they met at a local social evening.

'Sorry to mention it, Mrs Briggs,' said the butcher. 'But you owe me quite a few quid for the sausages.'

'But I haven't had any for weeks!' protested the good lady.

It turned out that Kim was smarter than they thought. He had been bringing in pieces of plain paper.

How do you demand an excuse from a dog?

* * *

'Why do you keep hitting me with a whip?' said the horse to the Jockey. 'There's no one behind us!'

* * *

The husband was phoning through an advert to the local newspaper.

'£2000 reward for lost cat.'

'That's a lot of money for a cat,' observed the editor.

'It's just to keep the wife happy. I've already killed it.'

* * *

'Sorry about your losing Fido, darling. I'll buy you a new hat.'

'If you knew how much I loved him, you'd buy me a fur coat!'

* * *

'Why did you kick that defenceless dog?'

'Defenceless! He lifted his leg – he was going to kick *me*.'

* * *

'What's happened to your dog?' asked Paddy's pal Mike. 'You took him t'school wicha every day when ye were only knee-high to a leprechaun – and den ye even took him to college wicha. Has he gone and died on ye, now?'

''T'was at college dere was de partin' of de ways,' sighed Paddy unhappily. 'The dog got his degree before Oi did.'

* * *

'Really, Mrs Prior! Why invite me into your house if you've got a dog who bites?'

'That's what I wanted to find out!'

*　　*　　*

'Is your Mummy or Daddy in?' asked the travelling salesman.

'Shouldn't come in our 'ouse, Mister,' warned the small boy. 'Me mum told me to keep me dog out because it's full of fleas!'

*　　*　　*

There's many a mother been called upon to explain when her innocent child witnesses the sight of two dogs indulging in gratuitous love. This excuse is as good as any:

'What are those two dogs doing, Mummy?'

'Well you see, dear, one dog is blind, and the other is pushing it to hospital.'

*　　*　　*

There occurs from time to time a peculiar concatenation of circumstances, in which the victims look around in vain to find the culprit; in the end they find there is no villain in the piece, and no excuses are offered. The following is a true story; only the names are changed to protect the innocent!

One morning Elsie opened a tin of salmon to make

sandwiches for Alf's lunch at the factory. Having a little left over, she scraped it on to the cat's feeding dish, knowing that her pet did not share the enthusiasm for cat food displayed in TV commercials by fellow members of its species, and had a taste for the odd delicacy.

Alf left for work. And she left to do some early morning shopping.

On her return, she found the cat's dish empty, and the cat dead on the kitchen floor. In panic, she called the Manager at the factory.

'This is Mrs Perkins,' she said. 'Will you tell Alf not to eat his salmon sandwiches? The cat's just eaten some and died!'

'I'll call you back,' said the Manager. A few minutes later he returned the call.

'Mrs Perkins? I'm sorry, but Alf was feeling hungry in mid-morning and ate the sandwiches, so we've rushed him off to hospital.' At the hospital, Alf suffered the agonies of the stomach-pump treatment, injections and saline drips. The treatment alone nearly killed him. Elsie made a fruitless trip to the hospital, as she wasn't allowed to see him, and returned home weary and worried and made herself a cup of tea. There was a tap on the kitchen door and the milkman looked in. 'Sorry about the cat,' he said.

'How did you know about it?' asked Elsie.

'He ran right in front of my float without warning and that was the end of him,' said the milkman. 'Didn't you see my note?'

Court without an Excuse!

'It has been proved beyond doubt that for the past two years you have been a bigamist,' said the judge, eyeing the culprit in the dock severely. 'You conducted a married life with one poor woman in Manchester and another in London. Have you any explanation at all for this extraordinary behaviour?'

'The motorway and a fast car, your Honour,' offered the prisoner.

*   *   *

'It seems to me to be a most extraordinary case to bring before the Civil Courts,' confessed the judge. 'Here we have a wife suing her husband for damages and negligence whilst being a passenger in their own car.'

'It appears, m'Lud,' explained the plaintiff's counsel, 'that the defendant was driving along with his wife, took a sudden turn, and shot her into the road. Instead of stopping, he appears to have continued to the nearest hospital emergency department and demanded to see an ear specialist.'

'Extraordinary!' muttered the judge. He turned to the husband. 'Any excuse for this?'

'I didn't know she'd fallen out, your Honour!' protested the husband. 'I thought I'd suddenly gone deaf!'

* * *

The doctor was up before the Medical Tribunal for a preliminary hearing on a malpractice suit.

The Senior Medical Officer leafed through the deposition and turned to the doctor.

'On the face of it, Doctor, imprinting a rubber stamp on the stomach of the young woman concerned seems a strange method of examining a girl in the third month of pregnancy! Have you any excuse for this extraordinary method?'

'All I said,' explained the doctor, 'was "when you can read what's on there without a magnifying glass, come back and see me again!" '

* * *

'Let's get this straight,' puzzled out the confused magistrate. 'You say that you were driving just outside Dublin when you were suddenly confronted by a man who appeared to be drunk, and that you unavoidably struck him and killed him.'

'That's it exactly, Sir,' nodded the motorist.

'And then, of all things, you decided to bury him!' went on the beak.

'Right again, Sir,' assented the prisoner.

'What on earth for?' gasped the magistrate. 'How did you know if he was even dead?'

'Well, he said he wasn't. But you know the Irish, Sir – they're all born liars!'

* * *

The motorist was brought up for dangerous driving and resorted to the ancient excuse for keeping his licence.

'But my livelihood depends on my driving, Sir.'

'So does the pedestrians',' snapped the beak.

* * *

'Haven't I seen your face somewhere else?' queried the judge suspiciously, as the next prisoner was placed in the dock.

'No, your Honour. It's always been right here on me shoulders,' chanced the old lag.

* * *

The classic cop-out was when the Jewish coroner declared that the Arab who was found stabbed two hundred times in Golders Green was the worst case of suicide he had ever come across.

*   *   *

'I don't think you can really duck out of this one, Sikes,' said the judge to a well-known swindler. 'Here in court are fourteen cases in which you've tried to pay off bills with unsigned cheques.'

'Well, you know me, yer Honour – I'm a modest man. I just wanted the donor to remain anonymous!'

Excuse me, Sergeant!

The Private in the Royal Army Catering Corps was on defaulters for completely ignoring the inspecting Captain when he made his rounds in the kitchens.

'You didn't even come to attention when it was called,' barked the adjutant. 'Any excuse?'

'It was like this, Sir. I was in the middle of a recipe, and it said "Don't stir for twenty minutes!"'

* * *

Lance-Bombadier Alastair St John Pugh proved to be the Regiment's crack-shot of all time. He could hit any stationary or moving target time and time again with unerring accuracy, and with any weapon. Soon, the Regimental Trophy Room bulged with cups won with his uncanny gift.

Trouble broke out abroad and the Regiment found itself in the front line.

'Put Pugh up front,' ordered the CO. 'That'll teach the enemy a lesson.'

When the attack came, Pugh stood squinting down his sights, apparently petrified.

'For God's sake, man!' shrieked the Sergeant, 'Why don't you shoot?'

'But Sergeant,' protested Pugh, 'there are *people* in the way!'

* * *

The Guards marched into the mouth of the cannon like the well-drilled machine they were. All except a Private.

'That man there!' called the Officer. 'What have you got inside your trousers? Splints?'

'No. Fear, Sir.'

* * *

Private Allsop was being court-martialled for cowardice in face of the enemy.

'You were ordered, Allsop, to fire at will. Why didn't you?'

'I didn't know which one was Will, Sir!'

* * *

The Sergeant scowled at one of the men on parade.

'You 'orrible little man, you!' he barked. 'You come on parade with your hair uncut, your boots unpolished and your rifle uncleaned! You're an 'orrible little Peruvian wart. What are you?'

'An 'orrible little Peruvian wart, Sarge!'

'Don't open your mouth when you're talking to me!' rapped the Sergeant. 'What's your excuse for such an 'orrible turn-out? Supposing we went to war all of a sudden, eh?'

'Well – when I looked in the paper this morning, Sarge, we hadn't been doing too well with Peru. I thought I'd better start showing who's side I was on!'

*　*　*

Officers can always be relied on for coming up with better excuses than the ranks. That's why they are Officers. Can you beat this one for sang-froid?

'Sir! A message has come through from HQ.'

'Very good, Sergeant. Read it out.'

'It's sent to you, Sir, Captain Frobisher. It reads: "To Captain Frobisher from Officer Commanding 41 Group. You are without doubt the most incompetent Officer I have ever had the misfortune to have under my command, and you are to relieve yourself of your duties forthwith and return to base." '

'Very good, Sergeant,' drawled the Captain, 'Get that decoded, will you?'

* * *

A local Danish fisherman was receiving special pay as a weather expert during a NATO exercise. For a whole week his forecasts had been spot-on. The Assault Group paraded at 06.00 for the final push. Weather conditions were all-important, and the fisherman was brought before the CO.

'How about today, Hans?' he asked.

'No know today,' the fisherman shook his head. 'No hear local radio.'

Excusellaneous!

The courier bellowed down the coach to the seated tourists.

'We are now passing one of the most famous brothels in Paris.'

'Why?' came a voice from the back.

*   *   *

The Moscow Returning Officer had no excuse to offer when he had to announce that next year's election results had been stolen.

*   *   *

The service was terrible. The man grabbed a waiter.
'I've only got an hour for lunch.'
'I don't want to hear about your labour problems!'

*   *   *

Mr Jones the bank clerk was disgusted with the next-door neighbours, and particularly with their dustbin, which permanently exuded the pungent odour of curry. He decided to complain, and went to knock on the front door.

'Yes please?' said the Pakistani.

'It's about your dustbin,' began Mr Jones.

'Oh, so sorry. There was a vacancy, but it's been let!'

* * *

Two pals were drinking in a pub, and one announced that he was emigrating to Canada at the end of the month.

'Just like all the others, eh?' jeered his pal. 'The rats always leave a sinking ship first.'

'It's not that at all,' said the other. 'When I was a kid, homosexuality was an offence. Now it's been made legal. I'm leaving before it becomes compulsory!'

* * *

'Mary, Mother o' Mercy! You've broken your mother's heart! Fancy carrying on wit a Protestant!'

'I said *prostitute*, Mother.'

'Thank the Lord for that!'

* * *

The middle-aged couple were going home after spending an evening with their neighbours.

'Every time you go there,' complained the husband, 'Freda is knitting. You'd think just for once she'd look after her guests – but there she sits, knitting and knitting. There's no excuse for that.'

'Well,' said his wife, sticking up for her friend, 'it does give her something to think about while she's talking!'

*   *   *

It was on a bus.

'You ought to be ashamed of yourself, a man like you not offering that young lady a seat – especially as she's pregant.'

'She's my daughter. And she's not married.'

'That's still no excuse.'

'She's been pregnant four times already.'

'That's still no excuse.'

'She never ate her rusks?'

*   *   *

They were driving home. She had maintained a tight-lipped silence for most of the journey but could no longer contain herself.

'Fancy interrupting the Chairman in the middle of his after-dinner speech! What possible excuse have you got for such behaviour?'

'I was just getting my own back.'

'Really! Supposing *you* were interrupted every time you opened your mouth?'

'See what I mean?'

*　*　*

Down at the pub they were all boasting about their sons' careers. 'I've got no excuse for young Ernie,' confessed his father. 'He's lazy, and that's it. If only he had a trade, then at least I'd know what kind of work he was out of!'

*　*　*

I've sent back the forms asking for my estimated income to the Income Tax people with no name and address on them. If they want me to guess how much I'm going to make next year, they can guess who sent it.

*　*　*

'Madam!' breathed the cop heavily, putting away his notebook. 'You've just involved me in a prolonged enquiry because you told me you'd been assaulted by a local boy, and I've found out that was thirty years ago! What excuse have you got for that?'

'Now and then I just like to talk about it!' she explained winsomely.

* * *

The guerrilla leader, in enrolling new volunteers to the Cause, put them through a rigorous test of commitment and fanaticism. Next in line was a poor-looking farmer.

'Are you prepared to give up every single penny you own for the Cause?' he asked.

'Yes,' came the prompt reply.

'Are you willing to sacrifice your wife and family as well?'

'Yes.'

'Are you willing to give up your house, your field, your ox, your ass, your chickens, your goat?'

'No.'

The leader rose up threateningly. '*No*? And why not?'

'I *have* a cow!' shrugged the man.

* * *

The new vicar's first parish was situated in a wild and remote part of Northumberland, and after a spell the bishop felt called upon to pay him a visit and see how he was coping. Unannounced, he sat at the back of the church and listened to the vicar's conduct of the service.

Afterwards he called upon him at the vicarage. 'This is a delicate matter,' he began, 'but I am afraid I must reprimand you for referring to Jesus feeding the five hundred. There is no excuse for such ignorance. It was of course five thousand.'

'Do me a favour, bishop,' the vicar retorted. 'This lot up here would hardly believe fifty!'

*　　*　　*

It's amazing how some people will instinctively grope for excuses even when they aren't required. Like when one housewife ran into an old friend in the street, and after the usual gossip she said, 'Have you seen what's been going on in Cambodia?' The other replied, 'We can't see a thing where we are – we live at the back.'

*　　*　　*

On the other hand, no excuse in the world can patch up the damage if it's too far gone. Like the young man who went into the chemist to make some necessary purchases – explaining to the chemist with a wink that he would be alone with his girlfriend that night, in her house.

'Her folks are going out to some stupid opera!' he laughed.

Later on, when he called at his girlfriend's house, the mother was waiting in the hall ready to leave. 'I'm just waiting for my husband to come back from work and you can have the place to yourself,' she assured him. 'Ah, here he comes now. I'll introduce you to him.'

'No need,' said the chemist, 'I happen to have three tickets for the opera anyway!'

* * *

'I never bothered to read your books,' said the ingénue haughtily, when introduced to the Professor at the cocktail party, 'because you had no excuse for refusing to join up in the war!'

'My dear girl – *I* was the Civilization they were fighting for!' he replied.

* * *

'After all the time I spent getting you dressed properly for the wedding, Mick!' complained his wife. 'And now you've gone and put your shoes on the wrong feet.'

'Dere de only pair of feet Oi got,' he countered huffily.

*　　*　　*

The husband could stand his wife's nagging no longer, and so one afternoon when she was out he packed his bags and went off and joined the Foreign Legion. After serving his twenty-year stint he'd had enough of the Sahara, and hoping that his absence might have brought about a change of heart in his wife, returned home.

'Where the hell have you been, then?' she cried as soon as he entered the door.

'I've been in the Foreign Legion,' he said.

'Blimey! What kind of licensing hours do they keep?' she barked.

*　　*　　*

'I notice you haven't bought me a birthday present again,' said the husband wearily. 'What excuse have you got this time?'

'I couldn't see a thing you'd like,' she explained. 'So it being your birthday, I spent £30 less on meself.'

* * *

He staggered upstairs to bed after a hard day working late at the office.

'Is that you, Jack?' murmured his wife from under the covers.

'Why? Who were you expecting?' he asked.

* * *

She was very beautiful and very prim, a typical product of a true-blue Tory 'county' family. It wasn't long before she complained to the Office Manager that there was far too much slap-and-tickle indulged in by the male members of the office. 'On Friday when we were leaning out of the office windows watching the election parades, someone slammed the window down on me and assaulted me from behind!'

'Didn't you shout out?' said the Manager.

'What? And make everybody think I was cheering the Socialists!' she retorted.

* * *

The landlord at the local pub was always in trouble with his wife for some reason or another. If it wasn't for drinking the profits with his cronies, it was for hiring, and flirting with, dolly barmaids. But years of practice had made him adept at excuses and he invariably got himself off the hook. Early one evening an expert ventriloquist appearing at the local Club entered the pub, with the dog he used in his act.

As it happened, he wanted to replace the dog as it was getting old – and had figured out a way of doing it.

'What will it be, Sir?' asked the landlord.

'Gin and tonic,' said the vent.

'Make mine a whisky,' said the dog. The landlord served the drinks, not quite believing his ears.

'A little drop of water, if you don't mind,' said the dog. 'Thanks. Now just a touch of ice. That's fine. Do the honours, will you guv?'

The ventriloquist picked up the drink and poured it down the dog's throat.

'That hit the spot,' said the dog. 'Another one please, landlord.'

After he served the drink, the landlord whispered to the owner. 'You know – a talking dog like that would improve my custom no end. How much do you want for it?' The transaction was agreed upon, the ventriloquist took the money, drank up and patted the dog as he left.

'He's your boss now,' he called to the dog.

'You rotten swine,' growled the dog. 'Just for that I

won't say another word in my life.' An hour later, the landlord's wife wanted to know why the till was £50 light.

We are still waiting for the landlord's excuse.

*   *   *

The American had heard that all dogs taken into Britain had to be put in quarantine for six months. He provided himself with a white stick, put on dark glasses, and a guide-lead on his dog. As he passed through British Customs, the Immigration Officer said to him, 'It's not usual to see a Yorkshire terrier as a guide dog, Sir. They're usually Alsatians.' 'You mean it *isn't*?' gasped the man in surprise!

*   *   *

The pub was getting crowded.

'Here! What's your hand doing on my wallet?' a customer challenged the thief.

'I'm sorry. Since I've given up smoking I don't know what to do with me hands!'

*   *   *

'No! No! *No*!' shrieked the choreographer dementedly to the heavily-built lass with the two left feet. 'Can't you hear the piano?'

'Oh yes! But it doesn't bother me!' she said brightly.

*   *   *

Lady Parkington-Smythe was collecting donations towards a good cause. She called on a local speculator, reputed to be a millionaire.

'I'm sure you'll agree with me that someone as well-provided as yourself ought to give a handsome donation, bearing in mind that others less fortunate have given generously.' The man explained to her that people tended to forget that he had four ex-wives who demanded money continuously, grandparents, and a host of grandchildren, who constantly asked for support – not to mention relatives abroad.

'I beg your pardon,' apologized her Ladyship. 'I didn't realize you had to give away all that money.'

'I don't,' said the speculator. 'But you don't think I'd give money to strangers when I don't give it to my own relatives, do you?'

*   *   *

A famous cat-breeder reported the loss of a world champion blue Persian to the local police, offering £10,000 reward. The next day, the Inspector entered the station to allocate the various duties and found the place empty.

'Where is everybody,' he asked the Sergeant.

'They're all out looking for the cat!' was his reply.

* * *

The rabid left-wing agitator was standing on his soap-box at Hyde Park Corner, haranguing an audience of precisely one. Just the same, the politico kept going, because the man was clearly a perfect victim of capitalist exploitation – down-trodden, undernourished, and wearing dirty old clothes.

'Just look at 'em all out there!' yelled the speaker, pointing across to Mayfair. 'Living in their big fancy hotels, driving their Rolls-Royces! There's no excuse for it! People like you and me must unite, comrade! Unite and chuck 'em all out! Why should they have the caviare, and we have the prunes and custard?'

'But I *like* prunes and custard!' said his one-man audience.

'Who the hell's talking to you!' yelled the agitator.

* * *

The Income Tax Inspector was not satisfied with a claims form sent in by a travelling salesman.

'I see that you've been provided with one of these new electric cars,' he began. 'My staff have gone into the matter. It's possible to travel from London to Edinburgh on as little as £10 worth of electricity. Yet you have claimed £10,000 a year expenses.'

'Quite right,' replied the salesman. 'It costs £6000 for the flex alone!'

* * *

The local cricket captain was persuaded to include a Cambridge rugby blue in his side for prestige purposes. The captain clouted the opening ball smartly to cover-point, and called for a run. The blue sent him back and the captain was run out.

'Sorry about that,' said the blue. 'But I'm a little stiff from rugby.'

'As far as I'm concerned,' snarled the captain, 'you're a big twit from Cambridge!'

* * *

The director called the actor over as the latter strolled on to the set.

'Listen,' he said, 'you're the stand-in and you're supposed to be dressed exactly the same as the star. Why are you wearing wellington boots?'

'I don't know what I've got to stand in yet, do I?' responded the other.

* * *

The young lady evangelist rattled her collection box among the crowd. 'Give for God!' she encouraged. One old boy stared at her obdurately, with hands firmly in his pockets. She smiled at him. 'Surely you have something to give to the Lord?' she asked.

'How old are you, young lady?' he asked.

'Nineteen.'

'I'm eighty-three. I'll be seeing Him before you, and I'll give it to him personally!'

* * *

Jesus went out into the wilderness and called upon God to allow him to perform another miracle.

'Oh, not another one!' complained the Father.

'I just want to walk across the Sea of Galilee,' explained Jesus.

'Why?'

'Have you seen the price of the ferry?' said His Son.

* * *

The man thumbed the Queen's car down on a wild, rain-lashed part of the country and begged a lift. 'I'm afraid protocol forbids it,' said the Queen. 'There is no precedent.'

'But if you recall, Your Majesty,' said the man, 'In 839 AD, Queen Boadicea drove all the Romans back!'

There's no Excuse for these Jokes!

The dinner-party had been a great success, but the food had been rich and the guests confined to their seats for a long time. As a result one of the male guests was fighting a losing battle with acute wind. Able to contain himself no longer, he gave vent to a wall-shaking blast. There was a moment of embarrassed silence. The hostess, seeking any excuse to cover the incident, smiled all round.

'Seconds anyone?' she offered.

* * *

Every golf club has them. That is, a small côterie of vinegary lady members, devoted solely to making complaints and exerting their authority as founder-members. This particular group had run through the card – complaints about the condition of the course, breaches of golfing etiquette, the short-comings in the locker-rooms and the food, had all been passed on to the harassed Secretary, and the ladies were now running short of ideas.

'I think,' said one, as they sipped afternoon tea after a game, 'that it's disgusting that there are no tongs in the sugar. With all those men visiting the toilets and not washing their hands, tongs really should be provided!' The rest of her cronies agreed, and the Secretary was duly summoned and the complaint passed on. But when they all checked the following week, there were still no tongs in the sugar bowl. They called the Secretary over.

'We thought you said you would see that a pair of tongs would be supplied?' they complained.

'But ladies, they are!' protested the Secretary. 'They're hanging in the men's toilet!'

* * *

'How do you get yourself out of this one?' groaned one feller to his pal as they sipped a pint at the pub. 'There was I, snuggled up to Veronica on the sofa, in front of a nice fire – the dog sprawled on the mat – discussing our wedding. The dog has a little scratch on its back. I said to Veronica, when we get married, you can do that for me! And by the time she turned round to look the blasted dog was licking its balls!'

* * *

The young man was about to go on his honeymoon cruise. To cover all eventualities he went into a chemist shop and asked for a packet of Durex and a box of sickness pills.

The chemist frowned. 'If it makes you sick, why do you do it?' he asked.

* * *

There's no excuse for bad language, although there are some who maintain that the game of golf is a justifiable exception. The Colonel always gave vent to his feelings on the course, and remained uninhibited by the fact that his present opponent was the bishop.

'Sod it! Missed!' he cursed, at his very first attempt at a putt. The bishop raised his eyes silently heavenwards. Later on, the Colonel made an air shot.

'Sod it! Missed!' he exclaimed.

'It's a great pity,' observed the bishop, 'that users of profane language are not struck down where they stand by a bolt from Heaven.' At that moment there was a loud clap, a dazzling stroke of lightning, and the bishop dropped to the ground. A deep rumbling voice from above echoed: '*Sod it! Missed!*'

* * *

The doctor was surprised to see a very young and fit-looking man enter his surgery.

'There doesn't seem to be much wrong with you, my lad,' he observed.

'It's my marriage,' explained the patient. 'I'm really worried that it's going to fall apart unless I can cure my troubles with premature ejaculation. Is there a pill I can take, or anything?'

'It's not a physical problem,' said the doctor, shaking his head. 'And I'm not a psychiatrist. But I've got a rule-of-thumb treatment if you want to try it. It's just a question of mind over matter.'

'I'm willing to try anything,' urged the young man.

'First of all, we need something in the way of a hobby, something of absorbing interest to you other than sex. For example – are you keen on any sport?'

'I'm afraid not.'

'Well, how about food?' suggested the doctor.

'Yes, I'm very fond of food – a bit of a gourmet, in fact,' the other replied.

'Good. Now what I want you to do, immediately you commence operations with your wife, is to run through your favourite five-course meal, and say it out loud. With a bit of luck, that will distract your mind enough to curb your sexual enthusiasm.' The young man shook his head.

'My wife is a very conventional woman. I don't know if she'll stand for it,' he muttered.

'It's up to you,' said the doctor. 'It might save your marriage.'

With this in mind, the husband determined at least to give it a try. In bed that night, as soon as he began intercourse, he gritted his teeth and said in a very loud voice.

'I shall commence . . . with a very cold . . . vichy-soisse . . . soup!'

'Stop that!' snapped his wife, shaking him. 'You know I don't like kinky sex.'

'With coffee to follooooooooooooooooow!' groaned the poor chap.

Excuses for all Occasions

There is an art in employing the right excuse for the right occasion. Sometimes the light-hearted quip punctures indignation; other times it produces a punch on the nose. It is entirely up to the excuser to choose correctly when attempting to appease the excusee! In general, the more elaborate excuses require careful preparation. If that isn't possible, ruthless post-excuse cover-up work may be necessary (bribing neighbours, threatening small brothers, blackmailing your pal, *etc.*). But don't take a sledge-hammer to crack a nut. Assess the importance of the excusee carefully. The police and the wife qualify as red-alerts, but bosses hardly even qualify for an excuse these days – especially if you are a union man. Unions have sanctified all excuses and turned them into laws (*e.g.* if you're caught slacking on the job, it's called victimization). The author accepts no responsibility for the failure of any excuses offered here: after all, you are the one who is up the creek, and only you know what size paddle will get you back!

Excuses For being late

'Sorry, I'm late' . . .!!

'You're lucky I'm here at all.'

'Didn't you get my phone message?'

'I know I'm late. Don't ask me why. Just *don't* ask me!'

'I didn't sleep a wink last night.'

'I fainted on the way.'

'I'm *always* late.'

'Late? Blast! You know what it is? It's these new digital watches. I've been taking the Stock Market prices as the correct time!'

Or . . .

'The big digit's fallen off my digital watch.'
'I overslept.' (*a good piece of one-upmanship if it's an evening appointment*)

'Wasn't it foggy over your way?'

'Sorry I'm late. I booked a long-distance business call to Adelaide for 9.00 this morning, and the damn thing came through just as I was walking out of the house.'

'I had to call in at the doc's on the way. I've had this back trouble, and this morning when I got up . . .'

'Bloody wife left the car in gear and I went straight back through the garage doors.'

'I'm sorry I'm late – it's all these Russian trawlers . . .' (*and other non-sequiturs ad lib*)

On being out so late that you won't get home until the early hours of the morning: Book two nights at a local hotel. Send a telegram to your wife as if sent by kidnappers demanding a ransom (remember not to sell yourself cheap!). Turn up two days later and tell your wife the story of how you escaped. (An added touch is to come home by cab. On the way, throw out your jacket and trousers, and enter the house in your underwear.)

Excuses for debts, Non-payment of

'Oh by the way Fred – remind me sometime I owe you five quid!'

'I owe you ten quid? So *that* was it! I tied a knot in my handkerchief to remind me and couldn't remember what it was for. I've mended the washer on the kitchen tap; repaired the spare tyre in the car; invited some friends round for an overdue dinner-party; bought the wife an anniversary present just in case it was that, and booked a Super Apex fare for next year's holiday! Don't lend me any more money, Charlie – it's too exhausting!'

'A quid was it? Sorry! Here you are. I always used to tie a knot in my handkerchief, but since they've brought out tissues – I *must* find another system!'

'I don't know how I forgot! I wrote "Owed to Reg" right across the pound note as soon as you gave it to me!'

'Can you remember what I owed you?'
'Five pounds.'
'Make it ten and I'll pay you back Friday.'

'How much do I owe you? £375? What for? Oh the deposit on our holiday! I'm terrible that way. I pay back debts to miserable bastards straight away, and forget what I owe to the decent blokes!'

'Will a cheque do? Good . . . Oh damn! I've changed my suit.'

Excuses for Non-payment of bills

Write a letter in your left hand (if right-handed!) as follows:–

'Dear Sir,

I'm sorry about not paying your bill of £1264 for work done on house. I am in hospital undergoing tests. The doctors don't know what it is yet. I will see to your matter as soon as I'm fit.

Signed for Mr Potter on his behalf,

J.Seabrook (Nextdoor neighbour)

If it is a bill from *any* Ministry department, or nationalized industry, write as follows:-

'Dear Sir,

I am in receipt of your bill to the amount £29.75, but am querying the actual figure. According to my understanding, this amount should be £25.74.

Signed *etc.*'

All civil service departments must reply to letters, and you can keep this query going until inflation reduces the bill in actual money terms to about £10. With luck, as no civil service department keeps its personnel longer than ten minutes, and thus each new clerk has to pick up the correspondence from where it left off, delays will be so long, that your bill will be reduced in effective cost to about £5 by the time you agree with their figure.

On forgetting wife's birthday

'I thought at your age you'd appreciate it more if I *forgot* your birthday!'

'Dammit! I spent all my lunch hour looking for a present, and then left it at the office!'

'I haven't forgotten, darling. I planned a meal out and an evening at the theatre to see (*Name a hit show*). But I couldn't get the tickets until next week. Do you mind darling? Is next week OK?'

Post an unsealed letter addressed to your wife any time in the year; smudge the post-mark when it arrives, keep it in reserve. Slip birthday card inside it at last minute and throw it on doormat.

If your wife bursts into tears and accuses you of forgetting her birthday late in the evening, frown, say, 'I can't understand it,' phone your best pal and ask, 'What happened?' He's bound to think you're talking about something else, so just say, 'I see,' and ring off. Then explain to the wife that George and Freda were due to come round with *your* present and a bottle of booze and make it a surprise party; you've just phoned, and they can't get the car started. Next day, phone your pal, square him up, tell him to say he didn't even tell *his* wife so it would be a nice surprise for her too, and the reason they didn't come was he thought it was the next night. Buy the present the

same day. Give it to George before coming home.
Invite them around again that night.

*Note: This excuse is only worth the trouble if you are
newly-married and still in love.*

On forgetting wedding anniversaries

If it is your *first* wedding anniversary, clutch your
stomach, collapse, allow yourself to be put to bed
while you mumble about the fish you had for lunch.
Ask your wife to send for the doctor. When he examines
you, confess. He's forgotten anniversaries himself,
and he'll understand.

'Fat lot our marriage means to you! Wives *always*
remind their husbands about their anniversary!'
(*Suitable for all wedding anniversaries between the second
and twenty-fourth*)

Silver Anniversary.

There is very little chance that the average husband
will forget his Silver Wedding. But if by any chance
the wife has prepared it all in secret and you have
forgotten to buy her a present, confess to her that
you've just been fired from your job and claim that
the worry drove it out of your mind. In bed that
night, when all the guests have gone, gently suggest
that your boss is a bastard for firing you on your
Silver Wedding day. Your wife will agree with you

that you should confront him with this sentiment and ask for your job back.

Next day, come home and tell her that it worked, and that the boss has taken you back.

(*Note: Never let her meet the boss*)

(*Note: If you are self-employed – just grovel*)

Golden Anniversary

If the wife bursts into tears and says 'You've forgotten our Golden Anniversary!' just say 'Oh, to hell with it!' After all, you're going to die first and she's going to live off your insurance.

Excuses if your wife finds lipstick on your collar

'So what's lisptick on my *collar*? Time to worry is if you find it on anything else.'

'It's your lipstick.'
'No, it isn't. I never use that shade.'
'Isn't it time you did?'

'Take no notice, darling. It's the office spinster. She can't get a man, so she gets her revenge by clutching anything in trousers and putting lipstick on their collars.'

'I went into the big store to get some of your favourite perfume, dear. They didn't have any, and the stupid girl assistant tried to flog me their new unstainable lipstick. She put some on my collar as a demonstration and then it wouldn't come off. Said it was the material or something. Anyway – they promised me a new shirt if I went back tomorrow.' (*Don't forget to buy the new shirt next day!*)

If you are over fifty-five, don't make an excuse to your wife. Tell her you left it there purposely just to prove that you haven't lost the old charm. With luck, you'll find she'll try harder in bed that night.

Excuses for arriving home drunk

'I went back to the boss's place to discuss my promotion. Guess what? He's into wine-making!'

'Drunk! Of course I'm drunk! Do you know who I ran into? You're old flame Percy Trubshaw! And he still thinks I'm no good for you, and wanted to come round here and make love to you. I had to get him plastered quickly to put his mind off it – *somebody* around here's got to look after your good name!'

If you get drunk with a pal:
Go back to your pal's wife. Take the entire blame for getting her husband drunk and beg forgiveness. Get him to tell the same story to your wife.

'A cup of coffee or something, dear – quick! I had such a raging toothache I had to call into the dentist,

and it was so bad he gave me a shot of pentothol – I
feel so woozy!'

For arriving home drunk, late, and having been in a fight

You're in trouble.

This kind of situation requires a prepared excuse.
Proceed as follows:

Get one of your drinking cronies to write a note in
his own hand. On arriving on your front doorstep,
ring the bell and then lie down flat on the front lawn.
(In your condition, this shouldn't be difficult.) Pin the
note to your chest. The prepared note should read —
thus:

'Dear Missus,

Your husband entered a drinking contest at
the pub to win the money to buy you a present.

He won the money and we followed him home
and mugged him for it. Don't blame him, he
only did it for you.

Signed,

The Muggers'

'I know I'm drunk, dear, but let me explain . . .
Y'see – we had this feller round from the National
Federation of Business Ethics and he reported back to
the Board that business efficiency in offices dropped

off 50% after lunch because too many executives got drunk in the lunch hour, see? And he did this demonstration in front of the whole Company, see? And he took one feller and gave him a three-course meal and one glass of beer. Then they took this other feller – I mean, they both volunteered, like – and gave him a pickled egg and ten glasses of scotch – and then tested them both on a computer console to show that the feller who'd had all the booze was less efficient than the other feller.'

'And I suppose you were the feller who volunteered to drink all the scotches, and that's your excuse for being drunk!'

'G'lord no! But he proved his point you see! From now on I'm getting pissed *after* work!'

Arriving home smashed out of your mind

No excuse will get you off the hook in this case because you will be too drunk to remember it, and even if you did, you wouldn't be able to say it. If you're foolhardy enough to open your mouth (if the wife hasn't already guessed from the way you tried to smoke a cheese straw and eat a cigarette while chatting to the hat stand), avoid the letter 's' as it is a dead giveaway, or only say things with 'sh' e.g.

'Went *sh*opping in *Sh*epperton for a tin of *Sh*ellac ran into old Reggie *Sh*arp and had a few *sh*andies . . .' *etc.*

Employees of commercial companies might try:

'Got waylaid by a gang from our rival company; they forshed drink down me to try and find out our secret ingredient!'

If it doesn't work, don't worry too much. You will pass out very shortly after such an effort of concentration.

Parental excuses for kids' misbehaviour

'I don't like to say this, Mrs Baker, but your son Raymond made a terrible mess on my walls and carpet when he came in to play with my son the other day.'

'I blame these television commercials on cleaners, I really do! Kids watch them and think they *have* to make a mess of the place so Mum can use her new power-packed cleaning fluid!'

'Your little daughter came out with a *very* rude word at our Candy's birthday party, Mrs Jones. I thought I ought to tell you.'

'Good Heavens! What word?'

'Well, I don't like to repeat it . . .'

'No, please tell me and I shall punish her.'

'In that case – she said "bollocks".'

'Oh, Ha ha! *That* word! (*Or whatever rude word is quoted.*) No, you see, it's a technical word, funnily enough, which my husband has to use in his job. Bollocks are *carpentry joints*, *flange pipes*, *overseas shareholdings* . . . (whatever your husband's job is) and she hears him using it on the phone!'

'Your kid has plastered "bum" right across our front wall!'

'Well, I suppose for a twelve-year-old it could have been worse.'

'I'm afraid your little boy had a nasty accident at the party, Mrs Graham!'

'Oh dear! I am sorry. I tell him time and time again to say he wants to go, but he gets so excited he forgets.'

'He told my Julia he was going to do it before he did it!'

'At *last* he's remembering!'

'Good morning. Mr Ede? I'm Mr Franklyn from down the street. My daughter's been telling me that your son has been trying things on with her. I hope you've got some good excuse for his behaviour!'

'Hmm. Well, I know young Denis is at the curious stage and he's trying to find out what it's all about.

You say he tried to play around with your daughter and she stopped him?'

'Exactly!'

'I should have a word with her if I were you, Mr Franklyn. My son may be trying to find out, but she obviously already knows!'

'My young daughter told me that your son seduced her on the way back from school yesterday!'

'Ye-e-s? I'm not the chap to speak to, really. I should have a word with the Director of Biology at the school. Some pupils are at a more advanced stage than others!'

'I had a little heart-to-heart chat with my Teresa last night, Mr Williams, and she told me in confidence that your young Tom seduced her!'

'I see. Look, why don't you come round tomorrow night and we'll discuss it?'

'Why tomorrow night?'

'I've got the Hazells and the Peggs and the Barclays coming round tomorrow night. And according to my son, your daughter said that their sons seduced her as well!'

'My daughter is pregnant! And she says that your son is the father!'

'He's not a father *yet*! She's got to do her bit first!'

'My daughter is pregnant! And she says that your son is the father!'

'Thank God! I thought he was queer!'

'My daughter is pregnant! And she says that your son is the father!'

'I bet your relief is overwhelming. Come in and have a drink.'

'My daughter is pregnant! And she says that your son is the father!'

'That's funny . . . The wife and I were talking about families and so on only last night. And we both agreed that if we *had* to have in-laws – you'd be perfect!'

Excuses for being found in a compromising situation with a member of the opposite sex by your beloved spouse

'The only time I've ever felt the seven-year itch and *you* walk in!'

'You always said it couldn't be done this way, didn't you, smarty-pants!'

'It only proves you're right, dear – I *am* over-sexed!'

'Just rehearsing for my next marriage!'

'How did you manage to switch the light on from where we are, Miriam! Miriam? Good Lord! You're not Miriam! Where's Miriam? Miriam!! How come you're over there switching the light on when I thought you were here, Miriam?'

'No excuse, dear – deep down, I always thought you preferred to watch!'

The final excuse for marital infidelity is offered on behalf of the Women's Liberation Movement. We can now expect that wives will be found in embarrassing situations as often as husbands. Let us take the situation where the husband discovers his wife in bed with a lover. Provided the duck-out-from-under has been carefully rehearsed, 100% success is guaranteed:

'Eleanor! What's the meaning of this? In bed with another man?'

'Huh? . . . Oh, it's you, Harry.'

'Yes! It's me! Harry! Who is this man?'

'Never mind who he is. I'm sick and tired of your jokes about me. You always said if I went on the streets I wouldn't fetch ten quid. Well, there's my price, Harry! (*She waves cheque from under pillow.*)

'Ten thousand smackers!' (*The lover then snatches the cheque out of her hand.*)

'There was nothing in the deal about being interrupted by your old man! The deal's off!' (*He tears up the cheque, jumps out of bed, grabs his clothes and exits angrily, pausing on the way out only to say to Harry . . .*)

'That's the trouble with making deals with wives who are secretly still in love with their husbands! They always let you down!'

The Excuse Book of Medical Terms

Are you constantly having to find excuses for your bad personal habits, anti-social behaviour and general abnormalities? Perhaps there is a medical explanation which will silence your critics and save you the embarrassment of inventing stupid excuses and making lame apologies!

Consult our dictionary:–

Breaking wind (Medical term: *Slackorrhea*) An incurable condition caused by being born with loose anal muscles.

*   *   *

Catsneutia (Greek: *Katsnutia*) Desire to neuter cats. Also to throttle neighbours' pigeons and kick their whippets. The cure is to remove the patient from the source of the irritants.

*   *   *

Disorientation   A temporary spasm in the medulla oblongata region of the brain, inducing a confusion in time, place and action. It accounts for me pinching girls' bums, and for little boys saying 'bollocks' in mixed company.

*   *   *

Drunkenness   A virulent form of agraphobia: An overwhelming desire to escape from open places and seek the confined protection of (for example) a saloon bar.

*   *   *

Flashing   (Medical term: *Inverto-Hedonism*) A chronic conditon in which the sufferer is dominated by the need to share his pleasures with every passer-by.

*   *   *

Fornication An incurable disease caused by an excess of chromosome C.45 over hormone D.90 in the lymph. Daily injections bring relief and temporarily prostrate the over-active gland. (See also *Limp Lymph*)

*   *   *

Homosexuality A form of 'imprinting'. That is, the first thing the new-born sees is the doctor, and thinks that he is his mother.

*   *   *

Lateness Dr Ernst Frananburg calculates time as 10^{-24}, the rate of molecular change. But this varies in individuals. Hence some victims live their lives permanently two hours behind everybody else.

*   *   *

Nose-picking (Medical term: *Frigor Digitus*) A tendency for the tip of the forefinger to suffer frostbite and seek unconsciously for protection.

*   *   *

Overweight   Unfortunate side-effect of taking pills to reduce appetite.

*   *   *

Smelly feet   No medical explanation. Franz Svensson-son, leading world Chiropodist, opines that this is nature's way of drawing attention to the body's extremities and thus preventing their neglect.

*   *   *

Smoking   An addiction voluntarily indulged in by dedicated believers in lung cancer research.

*   *   *

Stuttering   An acute condition induced in the victim when searching for an excuse.

*   *   *

Swearing   Prescribed therapy for relieving cerebral tension and anxiety complexes.

*   *   *

Temporary Amnesia   A normal and not a pathological condition, caused by periodic regrouping of blood cells and neuro-electric impulses in the cerebellum It accounts for forgotten birthday gifts, anniversary celebrations, debts, *etc*. *etc*. No known medical antidote.

A CHILD IN THE FOREST

Winifred Foley

'A winner . . . a vivid and personal story of the life and
hardships faced by a Forest of Dean miner's family in
the 1920's . . . a moving commentary on the Forest way
of life as seen through the eyes of a child'
Gloucestershire Life

'A land of oak and fern, of secret hill farms and plain,
matter of fact market towns . . . Still a Forester, Winifred
Foley recalls vividly but unsentimentally the loving,
poverty-stricken home where she was brought up'
Birmingham Post

'Warm-hearted and well-observed' *Sunday Telegraph*

'The story is funny and touching by turns' *Manchester
Evening News*

A CHILD IN THE FOREST is the book on which the
Radio 4 Woman's Hour serial of the same name and the
BBC 1 television film, ABIDE WITH ME, was based.

All Futura Books are available at your bookshop or
newsagent, or can be ordered from the following
address:
Futura Books, Cash Sales Department,
P.O. Box 11, Falmouth, Cornwall.

Please send cheque or postal order (no currency), and
allow 25p for postage and packing for the first book
plus 10p per copy for each additional book ordered up to
a maximum charge of £1.05 in U.K.

Customers in Eire and B.F.P.O. please allow 25p for
postage and packing for the first book plus 10p per copy
for the next eight books, thereafter 5p per book.

Overseas customers please allow 40p for postage and
packing for the first book and 12p per copy for each
additional book.